I0158951

For Eriko

Holly, Chantel, Michael, Mary & Katy

THE 7th DISORDER

By Rhea MacCallum

SYNOPSIS: A young woman's struggle to live begins with a spoonful of chocolate pudding

CAST OF CHARACTERS

(4 females, 1 male)

REBECCA (f) – late teens/early twenties, wears baggy jeans and oversized sweater. Uncomfortably thin. Recently admitted into the clinic. Due to her extreme medical condition she is irritable, insecure and at times not quite in touch with reality.

ROBERT (m) – 21 yrs. old, wears designer apparel. He is a fashion model accustomed to living, breathing and socializing with the elite.

JOANI (f) – late teens, but she carries herself like a ten year old, wears all black. Sporty but sophisticated. Wealthy Upper East Side type.

SYLVIA (f) – early to mid-twenties, attempts to look trendy but always misses the mark. Overweight child/teen who starved herself thin, but continues to feel like a fat little girl.

CAROL (f) – thirty, a counselor, prim and proper, slick, dress slacks and shirt. Not content with the direction her career has taken.

SET REQUIREMENTS

The dining hall inside an Eating Disorder Clinic. Large table, five chairs, two theatrical cubes

THE 7TH DISORDER
A PLAY IN ONE ACT

By Rhea MacCallum

Copyright © 2004 by Rhea MacCallum
All Rights Reserved

CAUTION: Professionals and amateurs are hereby warned that this
play is subject to royalty. It is fully protected by Peathraichean
Publishing, and the copyright laws of the United States. All rights,
including, but not limited to the professional, amateur, motion pictures,
recitation, lecturing, tabloid, public reading, radio broadcasting,
television, and the rights of translation into foreign languages are strictly
reserved.

This dramatic work is fully protected by copyright. No part of this
work may be reproduced, stored in a retrieval system, or transmitted in
any form or by any means, electronic, mechanical, photocopying,
recording or otherwise, without permission of the publisher. Copying
(by any means) or performing a copyrighted work without permission
constitutes an infringement of copyright.

Performance rights are controlled by Peathraichean Publishing and
royalty arrangements and licenses must be secured well in advance of
presentation. When applying for a royalty quotation and license please
provide the number of performances intended, dates of production,
your seating capacity and admission fee. Royalties are payable with
negotiation from Peathraichean Publishing. The right of performance
is not transferable.

Due authorship credit must be given on all programs, printing and
advertising for the play.

Published by Peathraichean Publishing
peathraicheanpublishing@gmail.com

Printed in U. S.A.
ISBN – 13: 978-0996693011
ISBN – 10: 0996693017

Visit the playwright online at: **www.rheamaccallum.com**
Photo courtesy of Scott Wynn Photography at: **www.scottwynn.com**

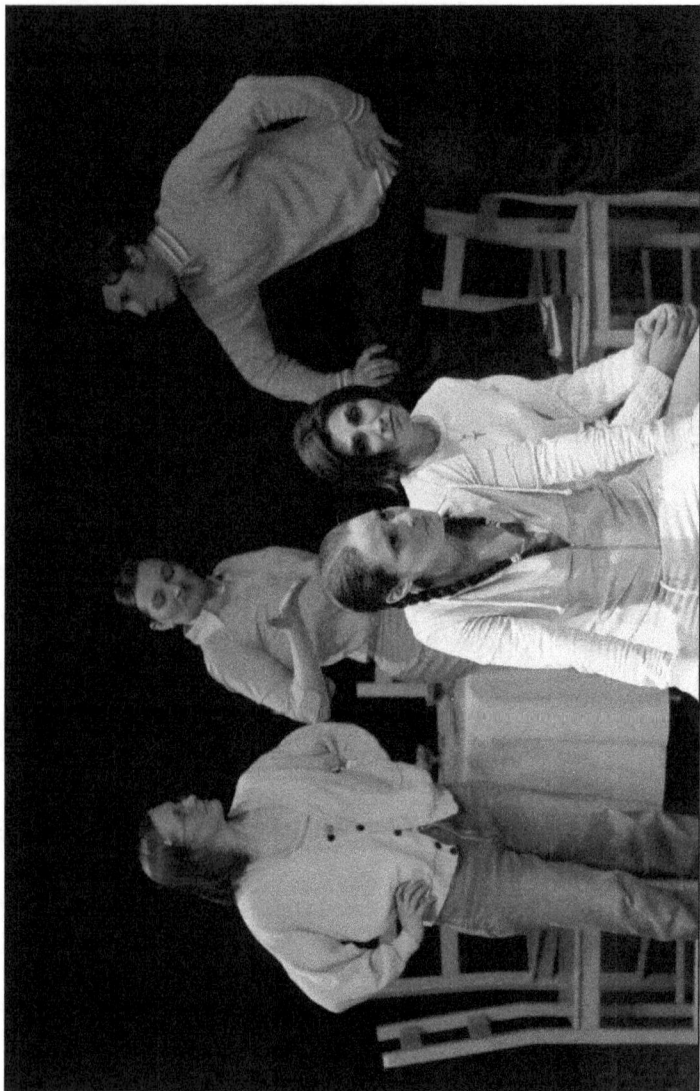

From left to right: Holly Lynn Ellis, Chantel Cherisse Lucier, Michael Raimondi; Seated: Mary Egan, Katy Gibbons

PROPS

Five parfait glasses filled with chocolate pudding
Five spoons

ACKNOWLEDGEMENTS

The 7th Disorder *was presented at Westbeth in New York City, March 17-20, as part of the Eighth Repertory Season of the Actors Studio Drama School at New School University. The production was directed by Eriko Ogawa with the following cast:*

SYLVIA	Holly Lynn Ellis
CAROL	Chantel Cherisse Lucier
JOANI	Mary Egan
REBECCA	Katy Gibbons
ROBERT	Michael Raimondi

Originally presented by TADA!, Janine Nina Trevens, Executive & Artistic Director, as a winner of the 2006 Annual One-Act Playwriting Contest and presented in the 15th Annual Staged Reading Series.

Monologues from this play have been published in JAC Publishing's "interJACtions: Monologues from the Heart of Human Nature, Vol. 2"

THE 7th DISORDER

AT RISE:
The four patients are seated at the table, staring at their pudding.
Carol stands, making sure everyone's been served.

CAROL: Okay, everybody ready? We all have our
chocolate pudding. *(Carol sits.)*
SYLVIA: *(Referring to Joani.)* She has more than me.
JOANI: Do not.
REBECCA: Can I say grace? *(Pause. They all react.)*
CAROL: Thank you, Rebecca, but it was already given
at the beginning of the meal.
REBECCA: I want to do it again. The pudding wasn't
at the table the last time.
ROBERT: Okay.
CAROL: If you want to say grace again, make it a silent
prayer.
JOANI: You're indulging her?
SYLVIA: It is her first day off the tubes.
JOANI: So, it's not that big a deal.
CAROL: Yes, it is.
ROBERT: Just cause you've spent the last five years in
and out of clinics doesn't mean-
REBECCA: Bless me father, for I will sin.

Rebecca stares hard at the pudding in front of her. The others are
stopped by her blessing and begin to eat. Robert puts his spoon
down between every bite. An attempt to prove he can eat without
binging. Joani plays with the pudding, licks it, takes her time.
Sylvia watches Joani and Robert, taking bites with them.

JOANI: Oh, geez, some people are so melodramatic.

ROBERT: You're one to talk. *(Sylvia giggles.)*

JOANI: *(To Sylvia.)* What?

SYLVIA: I didn't say anything.

JOANI: That's right, you didn't. Better keep it that way.

CAROL: Ladies, and Robert. Let's try to enjoy our chocolate pudding. *(Pause. Awkward silence.)* Can anyone remember the last time they had chocolate pudding?

SYLVIA: Last week.

JOANI: Yeah, they serve it every Thursday.

ROBERT: *(Indicating Rebecca.)* She wasn't asking us.

CAROL: Rebecca, what about you?

Rebecca shakes her head no. Pause.

SYLVIA: I can remember the *first* time I ate chocolate pudding too.

CAROL: Really?

JOANI: That's funny, I didn't think you could remember infancy.

CAROL: Joani.

JOANI: What!? I was joking.

CAROL: Sylvia was going to share something.

JOANI: It's not my fault she's fat.

CAROL: *(Carol moves to Sylvia.)* Joani!

ROBERT: She is not.

JOANI: She doesn't belong here.

SYLVIA: How would you know?

CAROL: We all have our reasons for being here, Joani.

SYLVIA: Yes. Yes, we do.

Shift in lights. To Rebecca, the others "freeze".

SYLVIA: Growing up I wasn't me, I was "the fat kid."
I wasn't a person. Just an object, described by an
adjective.
ROBERT/JOANI/CAROL: *(Chant-like.)* Fat fat fat fat
fat.
SYLVIA: By the third grade I figured out that no matter
what anyone tells you, it really doesn't matter if you're
smart, kind, funny, or generous, if you also happen to be
ROBERT/JOANI/CAROL: *(Robert, Joani and Carol close
in on Sylvia.)* Fat fat fat fat fat. *(Sylvia runs downstage pulling
Rebecca with her.)* Fat fat fat fat fat. *(They follow Sylvia
downstage, taunting.)*
SYLVIA: 'Cause when you're fat, you find yourself on
the receiving end of more cruelty than you even knew
existed.

*Carol pushes Rebecca away from Sylvia. Rebecca lands on the
downstage left cube. Carol, Robert and Joani push and torment
Sylvia.*

CAROL: Hungry, hungry hippo!
JOANI: Look it's Miss Piggy *(Makes oinking noises.)*
Where's Kermit, did you eat him?
ROBERT: Hey, hey, hey, it's Fat Albert! Lard ass!
(Kicks her ass.)
CAROL: Crisco butt!
SYLVIA: I learned that minding my own business
didn't help. *(Joani and Robert whisper a plot.)* Kids would
seek me out to ridicule and humiliate me. *(Robert trips
her, then high-fives Joani. Carol moves Sylvia to the downstage
right cube.)* And my mother's profound advice on how to
deal with it:

CAROL: Why not beat 'em to the punch line. Say something like,

CAROL and SYLVIA: *(They direct the end of the line to Joani and Robert.)* "I know I'm fat, but you're ugly and at least I can lose weight."

JOANI and ROBERT: So why don't you?

SYLVIA: So, I learned to live alone, inside my head. And food became my everything. *(Joani, Robert and Carol turn around one by one.)*

SYLVIA: My best friend, my lover, my mother. *(Walking to Rebecca.)* As I grew I became afraid to be seen because I knew looking up *(Looks up, sees Robert.)* Resulted in:

ROBERT: *(Robert intentionally running into her.)* What are you looking at, fat-so?

SYLVIA: And the worst injustice was knowing that the harassment came with complete impunity. If I responded angrily in self-defense, I'd hear:

JOANI/ROBERT/CAROL: God, you're so sensitive.

SYLVIA: *(Sylvia turns to face them, they move to the table.)* Until one day, I just couldn't take it anymore and I stopped eating altogether. The pounds simply fell away and I reached my goal weight. *(Sylvia walks back to her chair, followed by Rebecca.)* Only by that time I'd been fasting so long I didn't know how to stop. *(Sylvia and Rebecca sit as:)* And now here I am, still being told:

Lights back to normal. The others unfreeze.

JOANI: But, she is fat.

CAROL: Joani. Not the "f" word. You know better.

ROBERT: I think you're beautiful.

SYLVIA: Thank you.

JOANI: As if you're opinion counted for anything.

ROBERT: Excuse me?

JOANI: You don't belong here either.

CAROL: Joani. You are not the one who decides who does or does not belong.

JOANI: I was just being honest. You said we had to be honest.

CAROL: Honesty should always be tempered with thoughtfulness.

JOANI: Whatever.

CAROL: You owe both Sylvia and Robert an apology.

SYLVIA: No, really, that's okay.

ROBERT: No, it's not.

CAROL: Joani?

JOANI: *(To Carol.)* Fine. *(To Sylvia.)* I'm sorry. *(To Robert.)* Sorry. *(To Carol.)* There. Happy now?

CAROL: The attitude is not helping. Sylvia, you were going to share something.

SYLVIA: It was nothing. Never mind.

JOANI: *(To Robert.)* Just so you know, I'm not the only one who thinks you don't belong here. Rebecca thinks so too.

REBECCA: Do not!

JOANI: You said so just last night.

ROBERT: Well, that makes three of us then because I don't know what I'm doing here either.

SYLVIA: Then why are you here?

ROBERT: My agent's a paranoid freak, that's why.

JOANI: I thought you said your agent was supposed to be busting you outta here.

ROBERT: She is, she will. She's gonna call any day now, she could be calling right now. I actually need to get back to my room. *(He moves to stand, Carol cuts him off.)*

CAROL: You haven't been dismissed yet Robert.

ROBERT: Silly rules. *(He sits, Joani mocks him.)*

JOANI: Nice try.

CAROL: You don't have any idea why you're here?

ROBERT: None.

CAROL: What's at the top of your daily journal?

ROBERT: Well, I know what that says but-

CAROL: And that is?

ROBERT: I'm bulimic. But how can that be, it's completely absurd, I mean, I'm not even a girl.

JOANI: But you want to be.

SYLVIA: Ewww! That's so wrong.

REBECCA: Is that why you're a model?

ROBERT: You're one to talk, little boy. *(Everyone laughs and stares at Rebecca.)*

REBECCA: Stop it. Don't laugh at me.

JOANI: She wants to be a little boy!

CAROL: Joani, one more word out of you and you'll lose your TV privileges for the rest of the month.

JOANI: Noooooo! No.

CAROL: Don't tempt me.

JOANI: He started it. Mr. I Want To Be A Girl.

ROBERT: That's the most ridiculous thing I've ever heard. I don't model because I want to be a girl, I model because I'm attractive.

Shift in lights.

ROBERT: And I'm attractive because I'm, I'm careful. *(Robert escorts Rebecca to sit downstage.)* Careful about how I, how I operate, how I control myself, how I manage my energy. My body's energy. You don't understand what it's like. *(Takes off jacket/sweater, revealing runway apparel.)* To have to parade in front of a room full of gawking strangers.

Carol, Sylvia and Joani stand and join him, strutting as if on a catwalk.

ROBERT: And strut, strut, hips right, left, look sexy, make them want you. *(The women strike poses.)* This is serious business! If the clothes don't sell the designer won't hire you again. So you gotta, *(New pose.)* work it, *(New pose.)* work it. Make everything look good. *(Working the catwalk.)* Ignore the man in the second row who is fixated on your ass. *(Turn downstage.)* And again, *(Female models follow.)* strut, strut and turn and turn. Give 'em what they paid for. *(Female models strike pose. Robert speaks to Rebecca.)* The pressure is overwhelming. You have to be in top physical condition, always. So, I devised an exercise routine. *(He begins to walk in a circle.)* Every morning, pre-dawn walking, walking, walking. *(The others join him, one by one.)* Until the walking takes on speed. Faster, faster, gaining speed and I'm running. Running so fast I never want to stop. Just keep running, running. *(Mimes each of the activities named with others.)* At noon I venture to the gym, to play tennis or volleyball or basketball. Never leaving before three. *(Runs again. In place.)* Then, at night, another run.

Sylvia, Joani and Carol progressively fall back.

ROBERT: One mile, two, three. Five miles. Six. Eight. Ten miles. *(Sylvia stops running.)* I don't know how to stop. I can't stop. Running. *(Joani stops running.)* I have to keep. Going. *(Carol stops running.)* As long. As. I. Can. No matter how tired. No matter how weak. I must. Keep. Moving. *(Rebecca moves toward Robert as he collapses, but keeps moving/twitching.)* As long as there's energy in me. Energy to burn. I. Must keep. Moving. *(Rebecca touches Robert's arm, which calms him.)* It's what I had to do, to keep working. It's what I had to do to stay beautiful.

REBECCA: *(Reaching out to Robert.)* The Lord measures beauty by the heart.

ROBERT: For the Lord does not see as man sees. *(Stands up, gets jacket/sweater back from Rebecca.)* Samuel, right? Yeah, well everybody else measures beauty by what they see. *(Escorts Rebecca back to the table, seats her.)* Physical beauty increases your worth, and I am a valuable commodity.

Rebecca and Robert sit. Lights return to normal.

ROBERT: If all I wanted was to be a girl, why would I put myself through all this trauma?

JOANI: You tell me, *(Whispers)* big girl.

CAROL: What was that?

JOANI: Nothing.

SYLVIA: Liar!

JOANI: Mind your own business.

CAROL: Ladies, you're not making this any easier. It's Rebecca's first day on solids. *(Pause. They all eventually look to Rebecca.)*

CAROL: Remember how difficult your first day was? Do you? *(They all mumble or nod agreement.)* You could all be a little more supportive. *(Turning her attention to Rebecca.)* Why don't you try just holding the spoon for a while? Can you do that?

Rebecca tries, but can't.

ROBERT: Rebecca had a visitor today.
JOANI: Of course she did, she's new. Wait 'til you've been here a while. See who visits ya then.
CAROL: Rebecca, did someone come to see you today?
REBECCA: Yeah.
CAROL: Who was it?
REBECCA: My boyfriend.
CAROL: Oh, that must've been nice.
JOANI: Bet they had sex.
CAROL: Joani.
JOANI: What? It burns calories. *(Whispered)* I'd do it.
CAROL: That's quite enough out of you.
JOANI: Does that mean I can be excused, Carol.
SYLVIA: No way.
CAROL: You know the rules, better than anyone. No one leaves 'til everyone is finished.
JOANI: What about you? You haven't finished yet.
CAROL: I'm full, Joani. I don't need anymore.
JOANI: But that's not the rules, Carol. You have to eat everything too. If you don't have to, we don't have to.
CAROL: Joani. I'll be the judge of who is or is not finished and I am done. Nothing further to discuss.

Lights shift, spotlight on Carol.

CAROL: I don't have anything to say. I'm not a patient here. I'm normal. What? So, I'd like to lose a few pounds, that doesn't mean I have a story.

The others bang on the table, prompting:

CAROL: Okay, okay, fine. I believe in the great American dream. Female version. If you could only lose those last five pounds, then somehow life would be perfect. You'd suddenly become a new woman. A woman pursued by Ken doll handsome, wealthy men who shower you with bouquets of flowers and expensive jewelry. You'd be blond, five ten, wearing quasi-intellectual glasses, a man's oxford shirt in a sunny New York flat, sipping coffee while finishing the Sunday crossword puzzle. You'd drive a shiny red coupe and work in some great big city building where everyone's impressed with your very feminine but authoritative self. And in the evenings you'd go home and whip up a magical gourmet meal and eat three bites and be satisfied. You'd be a superwoman goddess, yes, you would, I would, will be. As soon as I lose those last five pounds.

Shift in lights.

CAROL: Now, if you'd all finish yours.
ROBERT: *(Indicating Rebecca.)* That could take a while.
CAROL: Then we'll wait.
JOANI: Aw, man. This is my night to call the station too.
SYLVIA: So what? There's nothing on TV anymore, but reality shows.

ROBERT: That's not reality.

JOANI: You're just jealous-

ROBERT: Please.

JOANI: -cause they're on TV and you're not.

ROBERT: Same goes for you, Little Miss I want to be an Olympic, gymnast, Mary Lou Retton, Nadia whoever, but I didn't make the cut cause I suck!

JOANI: That's not true.

CAROL: Ladies, don't you think we should-

JOANI: Take that back. I was good. One of the best. Isn't that right, Sylvia?

SYLVIA: One of the best.

ROBERT: Of course you agree with her, she sneaks you food.

CAROL: What? *(Robert feigns shock.)*

JOANI/SYLVIA: Nothing.

ROBERT: I've seen her do it.

JOANI: That is such a lie.

REBECCA: God's gonna get you. *(Robert laughs.)*

CAROL: Sylvia, is this true?

SYLVIA: No.

CAROL: Sylvia, you know our relationship is founded in trust. Any violation of that trust destroys the foundation of our relationship. You don't want to destroy our relationship, do you? Do you? *(Sylvia shakes her head no.)* Does Joani sometimes *(Sylvia looks at Joani.)* Sylvia! Sylvia, look at me. *(She does so.)* Does Joani sometimes sneak you some of her food?

SYLVIA: Maybe. Just once or twice. She doesn't like mashed potatoes.

CAROL: You know you're not allowed to do that. I'll have to report it to Dr. Apple.

SYLVIA: I'm sorry.

JOANI: *(Whispered, but not soft enough.)* I thought we had a deal.

CAROL: Joani, don't you want to get better? *(Joani nods.)*

JOANI: I am better now. Much better. *(Cheshire cat grin at Carol.)* Thinking I was fat, it was all in my head. I just got confused, obsessed over nothing.

SYLVIA: Joani, she doesn't have the authority to sign you out.

JOANI: I know, but I'm really much better.

CAROL: I'm sure you are dear. Now stop playing with your food.

Lights shift.

JOANI: Stop playing? But I like to play. And the gym is my playground. *(Joani steps forward. Gestures for Rebecca to follow.)*
It's where I turned childhood somersaults and cartwheels into Olympic medal dreams. My specialty: the balance beam.

Carol moves stage left cube to center stage. Robert and Sylvia stretch and prepare for workout.

CAROL: *(Russian accent.)* Hurry up Joani, let's see your new routine.

Joani begins balance beam routine by stepping up on cube. Robert and Sylvia mimic her moves.

JOANI: For years my natural talent carried me.

CAROL: *(Positive instruction.)* Straighten your back! Lift your chin! Focus!

JOANI: Then I grew three inches in six months and gained too many pounds. *(Joani falters in routine. Robert and Sylvia do not.)*

CAROL: Point your toes! You're balancing more weight now, Joani. Adjust!

JOANI: I'm trying Gordi! I'm trying. *(Steps off cube/speaks to Rebecca.)* One day I overheard Coach Gordeeva tell my father:

CAROL: Joani's a solid athlete, but she lacks that extra edge. She doesn't seem willing to do everything it takes. You understand?

ROBERT: I understand.

JOANI: If an extra edge is what I needed, an extra edge I'd find. Waiting for me in the medicine cabinet. *(Robert mimes handing her a bottle.)* In a little brown bottle. Ipecac syrup. Drop, drop and… *(Mimes taking it and vomiting.)* I found my edge. My scores improved and I was back on the road to the Olympics again. Until suddenly I started falling, stumbling, fainting. And every time I fell there was nothing there to protect me. My bones.

SYLVIA: *(Examining Joani while speaking to Robert/Carol.)* She has several hairline stress fractures in her right leg. Her landing leg. Calcium deficiency. Iron deficiency. Frankly, we don't think she's eating.

ROBERT: Of course she's eating. She has regular meals. Joani?

JOANI: I eat. You've seen me eat. I eat all the time.

SYLVIA: Not enough for an athlete in training. Are you anorexic? Bulimic? It happens to a lot of the girls.

JOANI: I'm not a lot of girls!

CAROL: It's okay if you have problem. It's not your fault.

JOANI: I don't have a problem.

ROBERT: What should I do?

SYLVIA: I can recommend some clinics, out-patient therapy.

(Sylvia, Robert and Carol temporarily freeze as Joani speaks to Rebecca.)

JOANI: Baby-sitters who didn't know what they were dealing with, so after treatment:

Unfreeze.

CAROL: I'm afraid she's back to her old tricks.

SYLVIA: And a few new ones. Must have picked them up at the last clinic.

ROBERT: But you recommended them.

SYLVIA: They can only do so much. Your daughter has to want to change herself.

Carol, Syliva and Robert freeze again.

JOANI: *(To Rebecca)* But I like what I'm doing and I'm not going to stop. Ever. *(Unfreeze. To Robert.)* I'm sorry dad. This is the last time I'll need treatment. Promise.

ROBERT: Promise?

JOANI: Promise. *(Robert/Carol/Sylvia return to table. To Rebecca.)* I'll hide it better next time, he'll never even know. *(Joani and Rebecca move back to the table.)* I can't come back here again. I'd sooner die. Better to die young, than live fat.

Lights shift to normal.

JOANI: See me eat. Enjoy eating. *(Licks the bottom of her bowl.)* I'm cured. Ready to go home.

CAROL: Dr. Apple will be happy to hear it. Rebecca, how are we doing with that pudding? *(She shrugs.)*

ROBERT: She hasn't had a single bite.

CAROL: Rebecca, do you think you can scoop out a spoonful? A small spoonful? *(Rebecca shakes her head.)*

JOANI: The table won't be dismissed until you eat it, Rebecca.

SYLVIA: Does she really have to finish the whole bowl?

JOANI: Man, I'm screwed. I knew I should have sat at table three.

ROBERT: Poor baby. No TV.

JOANI: Shut up.

CAROL: It's time to pick up the spoon, Rebecca.

REBECCA: I can't.

CAROL: Just try.

REBECCA: Not chocolate.

CAROL: One bite. There's not much there.

REBECCA: I've had enough! Too much.

SYLVIA: You haven't had any.

CAROL: Just one little spoonful. I won't make you eat the whole thing-

JOANI: Thank god.

REBECCA: No, don't make me eat it. Not the poison, the chocolate pudding poison.

JOANI: It's now or never.

REBECCA: Never. Nevernevernevernever, ever.

ROBERT: They'll put you back on the tubes.

JOANI: Force feed you.

SYLVIA: You don't want that do you? *(Rebecca shakes her head no.)*

CAROL: Just one bite, Rebecca. I'll let you go easy today. Just one spoonful.

REBECCA: I can't. Ican'tican'tican'tican't.

JOANI: Yes you can, and you must, especially if you want to get out of here.

REBECCA: I'm going to be sick.

JOANI: You are sick.

SYLVIA: Shut up!

REBECCA: I don't want to be here.

ROBERT: You think we do?

CAROL: Try holding the spoon. Get used to it being in your hand.

REBECCA: Can't touch the metal, it'll hurt my skin.

JOANI: We're waiting, Rebecca.

REBECCA: God, save me. Let me be with you. Be nothing with you.

ROBERT: Excuse me?

REBECCA: I want to lie on my bed, close my eyes and lift off, feel myself floating, hovering, outside of myself.

SYLVIA: Carol?

ROBERT: Whoa!

REBECCA: Get lost in the thought that nothing is real, everything exists as a product of my imagination.

JOANI: What the hell is this?

CAROL: This is very real, Rebecca. You are real.

REBECCA: We're dreaming our lives. I feel my heart pounding as I think: I'm not really here, I don't exist. It's too fascinating, the thought that you could just disappear, float away into the ether.

ROBERT: Oh no she didn't.

REBECCA: I've always wondered where I could go if my body didn't drag me back down to earth again.

CAROL: Food is nourishment, Rebecca. Imagine it's giving you strength.

REBECCA: You're trying to kill me.

CAROL: No, we're trying to save you.

SYLVIA: I know it's hard.

ROBERT: We've all been there.

JOANI: If you don't eat it, they'll make us sit here forever!

REBECCA: I can't. Just the smell of the cocoa fills me up. I don't need to swallow, I've already consumed it, fed the appetite. The hunger. *(Hits her stomach. Carol tries to stop her.)*
My stomachs bloated already, pushing out like a pork belly pig, hanging to my knees. Why won't it go back in?

ROBERT: There's nothing there.

CAROL: It's the disease, Rebecca. It's all in your head.

REBECCA: This morning I was light. I could feel myself lifting off, but you're making me heavy. Pushing me down. Way down into ground. Making me unholy.

CAROL: No, it's making you healthy, giving you life.

REBECCA: My body is the temple, temple of God. If any man defile the temple of God,

REBECCA and ROBERT: Him shall God destroy.

REBECCA: It says so in the Bible.

CAROL: Eating will build your temple. Don't you think God would want you to strengthen your temple?

REBECCA: I must stay pure.

JOANI: It's just chocolate.

REBECCA: Keep myself cleansed. I don't bleed down there anymore.

ROBERT: Ohmigod!

SYLVIA: That's amenorrhea.

CAROL: Maintain a healthy diet and your menstrual cycle will come back.

REBECCA: No, I'm pure now. It's a sign, He's chosen me.

JOANI: To do what?

CAROL: It's your body's way of communicating you're malnourished.

REBECCA: No. I'm pure. So pure God hurts me for even looking at, thinking about *(Shoves pudding away.)* Because when I do eat. *(Slams hand on table and buckles over in pain.)* Pain. Painpainpainpainpain. It hurts so much. *She rocks back and forth.)* Fire through my veins.

JOANI: We all know that pain.

ROBERT: Your body's not used to processing food.

SYLVIA: Keep eating regular meals and the pains will go away.

REBECCA: It'll go away, away.

CAROL: It's time, Rebecca.

REBECCA: It can't be time, can't be time, can't be time. I'm not ready. Nononono.

ROBERT: We're all waiting, Rebecca.

JOANI: Stuck here/ eat it.

SYLVIA: It won't kill you, I promise.

REBECCA: I'm sorry, so sorry, I -

JOANI: This isn't just about you, ya know.

CAROL: It's about everyone taking responsibility.

REBECCA: I I I, just, I don't think I can...

CAROL: Just one bite, Rebecca. It's time.

Fast black out on Rebecca, shaking as she reaches for the spoon.

NOTES:

www.ingramcontent.com/pod-product-compliance
Lightning Source LLC
Chambersburg PA
CBHW060607030426
42337CB00019B/3647